Painted Words

by

Walter Kemsley

for

Mary

Painted Words

by

Walter Kemsley

Rhapsody

Rhapsody
61 Gainsborough Road, Felixstowe, Suffolk
IP11 7HS

ISBN 1 898030 24 3

Copyright © 2003 **Walter Kemsley**
www.author.co.uk/kemsley

The moral right of the author has been asserted.

All rights reserved. No part of this publication may be reproduced, stored in a retrieval system, or transmitted, in any form or by any means without the prior permission in writing of Author Publishing Ltd.

This book is sold subject to the condition that it shall not, by way of trade or otherwise, be lent, resold, hired out or otherwise circulated without the publisher's prior consent in any form other than that supplied by the publisher.

British Library Cataloguing in Publication Data available.
Cover design by Louis Mackay
Drawings in book by the author

Printed in Kent
by JRDigital Print Services Ltd
Rhapsody is an imprint of Author Publishing Ltd

Dunwich Summer

Contents

1 **FOURTEEN LINES**
2 The Course Of Life
3 To My Wife
4 The Covehithe Road
5 **FROM THE NORTH DOWNS**
6 Flints On The North Downs
7 Dawn On The Downs
8 On The Medway
9 Estuary Fog
10 October On The North Downs
11 When Winter Whitens
12 The High Hills
13 Down from Downs
14 **LONGER NIGHTS**
15 Wet August
16 Hail In Late August
17 The Nip In The Air
18 The Straw Fires Burn
19 In Early Light on Frosty Day
20 The Lawns Deserted
21 November Puzzle
22 Closing Curtains
23 Autumn Dawn In The Woods
24 December Dawn
25 Dawn To Dusk, December
26 Nearing Christmas
27 February Thaw
28 May Morning
29 High Summer
30 **LA FRANCE**
31 To hosts in France
32 Undressing On The Beach At Cannes
33 Letters To Mougins
34 Autumn, Alpes Maritimes
35 November, Cote D'Azur
36 Nice Under Rare Snow
37 December 21st
38 A Mystery of Nature
39 **BIRDS, BEASTS & INSECTS**
40 The 'Only Birds'
42 Elegy For A Gannet
43 The Nest Abandoned
44 Farewell, Farewell
45 Birds and Leaves
46 The Turning Earth
47 Hard Winter
48 When Martins Leave
49 Snow In May
50 A Dog's Life
51 Morning Walks
52 To The Uttermost Forebear
53 The Fox
54 Heat Wave
55 Cold Gold
56 The Ant And I
57 Going and Coming
58 Flying Crooked
59 Requiem for a housefly
60 Not So Daft, Robert Graves
61 **THOUGHTS ON SUNDAYS**
62 Sunday Service
63 Harvest Festival
64 Christmas Day
65 Progress
66 Great Gifts
68 Churchgoing
69 Time
70 **WAR**
71 The Blitz
72 1945
73 Where Silence Tolls
74 After The Rhine
75 Chances

76 Grief's Sullen Hammers
77 From Normandy
78 Autumn Far From Balkan War
80 Time's Casualties
81 The Last Despatch
82 At The Time of Night Bombing of Cities
83 Greenham Common Protesters
84 Armistice Sunday
85 Brief Reunion
86 Veterans' Reunion

88 SUFFOLK

89 Suffolk
92 East Suffolk
93 May Morning, Westleton Heath
94 Adlestrop
95 I Remember Adlestrop
96 From Clamour to Curlew Call
98 Abbey Ruins At Minsmere
99 By Dunwich Shore
100 Thames Barge
101 The Fens in Winter
102 Spring Ploughing
103 Marshes

104 ODDS & ENDS

105 Weather Forecasts
106 The Lights Of May
107 So Idly Drifts the Severed Leaf
108 Out On My Walk
109 Knotty Problem
110 Night
111 Abandoned Line
112 Season Signals
113 Shopping In December

114 Costly Goal
115 Bottled Plums
116 Arts Council Grants

117 PEOPLE

118 Daughters And Mothers
119 Message To My Daughters
120 Stars in the Hedge
121 A Mother's Memory
122 Values
123 Beauty Borrowed
124 Young And Old
125 Ancestors
126 Waiting To See The Doctor
127 Looking At A Stately Home
128 Dogdays
129 The Fireside Men
130 In Bond Street
131 At Victoria Station
132 Darts Match
133 Commuters' Homeward Train
134 Man And Crow
135 If You Go Back
136 A Golden Day
137 Sunbathers In May
138 On Tankerton Sea Front
139 Country And Town
140 Looks and Feeling
141 Time's Legacy
142 Frank Woolley, cricketer
143 September
144 The Divide
145 What's To Come?
147 In Memoriam, E.B.
148 In Memoriam, M. W. E.
149 Thoughts In A Bath (or not T. S. Eliot)
150 Putting On Socks
151 The Octagenarian
152 01.01.2001

Suffolk Shore

Mary

Fourteen Lines

The Course Of Life

As on a river's course our lives must go.
Just as a tiny stream breaks from the earth,
So we come from the dark womb at our birth
And as a river widens, so we grow.
Our family, the children whom we know
In childhood, school, the chance friends of our youth,
Work, marriage, parenthood all shape our worth
As other streams affect a river's flow.

Our early rush and tumble are the stream,
Rocks, drought and driftwood symbols of the grief
Which all must suffer even when days seem
Joy's channels. Our broad reaches bear the leaf
Of autumn sluggishly, and finally
We enter death's unfathomable sea.

To My Wife

When I make up the balance sheet of age
Upon the debit side I find no lack
Of things to write. My ailments fill one page:
Skin blemished; eyes grown weak; a sagging back
Which once was straighter; legs with bulging veins;
A chest that grumbles when the winter roars;
And nights denied to sleep not through the pains
Of ardent youth, but by digestion's flaws
And shapeless worryings. To these I add
A catalogue of kindnesses not done,
Of skills unused and truths which I evade
For compromise; yet still you do not shun
The wreckage of the best that I could be,
And that alone saves me from bankruptcy.

The Covehithe Road

(*to an eroded coast*)

Beside the road, behind the hedge, below
The sky's white flock the shorn sheep move and graze
Where pale grass shifts and shadows come and go
To gentle rustling as a light breeze plays
Its summer airs. The roadside gardens glow
With plums and asters. Sparrows flock to ways
Rich in the harvest trailer's overflow.
Such days are children's endless summer days.

As if enticed by sirens to the sea,
The road winds on, like hope, till cliff tops bright
With stubble are its final company,
But that sea's waves, grown winter-hungry, bite
Their harvest from the sand cliffs' crumbling face.
The road, like life, ends broken off in space.

From The North Downs

Cornish Farm

Flints On The North Downs

The flints which lie about this earth-raw field
Have been turned over many times before:
Exposed, next hidden, next again revealed
As plough has led to harvest at the core
Of all our years. No wisdom can relate
What men disturbed them first and with what tools,
What others went to unremembered fate
And left no more than patterns of their toils.

But here, unchanging throughout every change
Of man and beast, crop, method and machine
Which makes familiar usages seem strange
And strange things commonplace, here flints remain,
As obdurate as childhood flaws and fears
Which break the surface of our later years.

Dawn On The Downs

From Downs first darkly grim
When night deserted them
But brightening with sun
I look as mist is peeled
From features of the Weald,
And slowly, one by one,
Trees, chimney, roof and field
Become again things known.

On The Medway

With red sail limp in summer airs
And water glinting at her bow,
With long sweep yellow as it stirs
Her black and red in blue below,
Sun-painted, she might even be
In fancy some spice-laden dhow
Reflected in an eastern sea,
And not the brick-filled barge she is
On laboured way to English wharves.

Estuary Fog

Fog moves across the mudflat shore
As time effaces memories.
It hides the mud from sea and sky,
Divides the seagull from its cry,
And adds bait diggers to its store
Of emptiness. Posts greyed by seas
Fade into grey they cannot stop.
Inland the fields become unknown.
Potato pickers in them pass
From sight, and leave me just the grass,
Sheep-bitten, on the sea wall's top
And island of myself, alone.

October On The North Downs

The gale spits rain on spikes of stubble
Where estuary gulls are down
To harbour from the grey sea's trouble,
And at the field's edge dock and nettle,
Jerked low, still cling to earth they own.

Rooks rising from the orchard's tangle
Like ink spots flung against the cloud
Will ride the wind, decide their angle
And to their ragged progress settle,
By gusts belaboured but not cowed.

When Winter Whitens

When winter whitens autumn's duns
Men put on sacks and take their guns
And stand like men in Brueghel scenes
To watch beside the skewbald greens.
The still air hurts. The land is dumb
Until mist parts and pigeons come
As spectre-grey as watchers' breath –
Thin ghosts which lack the seal of death.
Guns fire and cartridges drop red
To dirtied snow where firers tread.
A startled hare, no target yet,
Betrays its fright in silhouette.
The men reload and watch it go
Beyond the feathers in the snow.

The High Hills

The high hills have a happiness
For those who love to see
The sea stretch up to far skyline
Where ships come out of emptiness
And, growing from their first small sign,
Reveal their full identity.

The high hills have a happiness
For those who love to feel
The breeze come freely to the brow
And blow away all the strain and stress
While eyes absorb the space below,
Where seabirds glide and swoop and wheel.

The high hills have a happiness
When to the downward gaze
The river valley has revealed
Its silver ribbon of progress
By shadow-dappled copse and field
On briar-scented Downland days

Down from Downs

His great-grandfather cared for sheep
Where, green and bare, the North Downs sweep
Like waves up to the Kentish sky.
From lonely hut his ears would keep
Their keenness for the lambing cry.

His grandfather the hollow through
Would plough for sixty years. He knew
The chalk – stained earth curl from the share
Through autumn fallow to renew
The cycle of the crops grown there.

His father watched the ships come home
With grain the tint of honeycomb
And frozen mutton in the hold.
The mutton he made silver from,
The gold-brown grain he turned to gold.

He does not go to uplands bare
But in the town will drink and swear
And dice and wish that he was dead,
And when he gulps the dawn's clean air
Is when he staggers home to bed.

Longer Nights

Melton Park

Wet August

The night's rain lasting, ragged day
Crept like a beggar to the gate,
But there what gifts of harvest lay
Were uncut crops of dark drenched wheat,
And where cut ochre stalks were set
In green smears on a stubble floor
Hope's tombstones stood, neglected, wet –
The piled-up bales of barley straw.

Hail In Late August

In gardens where the roses' scent
Hangs heavy on the evening air,
And day by day on branches bent
The ripening fruit grows rosier,
And vegetable rows reward
Past labour, August's lessening light,
With man and nature in accord,
Slips hardly noticed into night.

In circumstances so benign
What other future could be guessed
Than tranquil passage of decline
With harvest stored and memory blessed?
But sometimes unexpected hail
Tears leaves apart and bruised fruit falls,
As plans are wrecked and high hopes fail
When death, the casual stranger, calls.

The Nip In The Air

One day at August's end the sun is late.
It is the morning when the mind is cleared
Quite suddenly of summer's opiate.
The eyes, no longer by the sun veneered,
Will see that in the stubble's long retreat
Of ochre rows green tendrils have appeared.
Bruised apples lie upon the grass still wet
From nightfall's dew, and mist damps old man's beard.

Along the valley where the hop poles rise
The mist has cut them down to half their size,
And, darker grown, the leaves of hedge and tree
Have lost with age their young variety.
The day is young; the sun will soon appear
But autumn's nip is in the morning air.

The Straw Fires Burn

The field is stripped,
The Dutch barn stacked with straw
And silence, and day's longest shadows fade.
There is no movement where the stubbles draw
The eye up to a skyline balustrade
Of dark trees which no ruffling airs explore.
Both hill and valley wait as if displayed
For ever where old books of hours restore
Dead years to life. The very moon seems stayed.

The toil of men and thrust of plants have gained
Their harvest haven here: the pure content
Which comes to runners whom the race has drained
Or lovers lying tranquil, passion spent.
But look! The moon is sailing from the barn;
Beyond the waiting hill the straw fires burn.

In Early Light on Frosty Day

Midwinter wears a powdered wig,
Disguising patchwork browns and greens;
The fur of frost chills blade and twig;
The nettle leaf reveals its veins
In channels through a surface grey;
Thin icicles make spikes on coats
Of ponies waiting for their hay
At paddock gates. Their grey breath floats
Into the shifting shoal of mist
While they stand still as seashore stone.
The birds puffed out on roosts resist
The claws of cold as best they can
Or shatter quiet with sudden flight
Which seems to shake the mist and show
A sun which apes a moon of white,
Aloof from this numb world below.

The Lawns Deserted

The summer chairs are taken in.
No teacups tinkle at the side
Of glinting water, and the thin
Bright chatter from the lawns has died.

The lawns are grey in mourning veils,
But, snug indoors, nobody grieves,
Though on the darkened current sails
Another scattering of leaves.

November Puzzle

In childhood's far November
When fireworks day was due
I chanted with young others
These age-old lines anew:
"Please to remember
The Fifth of November,
Gunpowder, treason, plot ..."
And wondered where the plot was
Where such strange trees all grew

Closing Curtains

The thin rain taps on browning bracken,
The acorns on wet tracks are brown,
In gardens dahlias, frost-nipped, blacken,
Late martins from our eaves have flown.

Not many weeks ago the yarrow
Made verges foam where stalks now stand
Stripped, brittle, brown. The grey days narrow.
Our lives draw in as nights expand.

Our curtains closed, we seek the pleasures
Which television screens unfold
While moonlight shows frost's silver treasures
Or dusk's cold skyline touches gold.

Autumn Dawn In The Woods

The dawn comes into autumn woods
At first like one unsure of words,
Grows fluent and with brightening ease
Slides glibly down the tall beech trees,
Lets loose its pattering tongue to coax
The last of gloom from crooked oaks,
And when the sky's faint stars have gone
Finds grounded stars to call upon
Where chestnut cases, opened wide,
Display four points and pale inside.
It shoos the wisps of mist away,
It tells the bracken's caves of day,
And with its final rousing words
Stirs up the hunting ground of birds.

December Dawn

The sharp frost shapes the blackbird's silhouette
But furs the last leaves lying on the lawn
In deadening silence of December dawn,
And, half aroused, I shiver and forget
That such a grey and frigid winter day
Conceals the heartthrobs of a coming May.

Dawn To Dusk, December

When autumn's last few gaudy beads
Are hung around the hedgerow's bones
And steps before night's frost recedes
Rasp leaves like waves on tide-line stones
And day's first feeble light becomes
The painter of the puddle's dawn,
Then hungry sparrows dart for crumbs
Before the feeding hands have gone.

Although a bright low winter sun
May soften frost to film of mud
Which shows earth greened with infant corn,
Bare hands may hurt with chilling blood,
For warmth and brilliance are not one,
And aches will still be in old knees
When evening's primrose streaks are drawn
And birds retreat to dark bare trees.

Nearing Christmas

Frost's silent knife upon last leaves
Has left them for the wind to down,
So that except where ivy cleaves
The hedges will be sober brown
And trees stand bare amid their loss
Like misers who have come to know
That hoarded wealth is only dross.
The pale snowberry waits for snow.

On frosty ground the village teams
Pursue the ball with charge and shout
Till early dusk bans all but dreams
Of goals or shots somehow kept out.
In market towns the Christmas treat
Is sought where decorations stand
And gaudy stores make us forget
The cold, hard beauty of the land.

February Thaw

Old stubble and young green have both appeared,
Thawed free of snow's cold uniformity,
But strips of snow stay in the hedgerow's lee,
Still frozen hard, wind-carved and not yet speared
By any stalks which winter's weight has spared.
A timid sun sneaks intermittently
Across the fields, and seems to shy and flee
As if snow's rearguard finds it unprepared.

Rich landscapes of the great Venetian school
Await their season while each threadbare day
Shows tiny items in the Flemish way.
Twig, ivy berry, sere leaf, ice on pool –
Sharp winter brings to eye details so small
And crusts of silence crack at one bird's call.

May Morning

The bugles of May are sounding reveille.
Come out sleepy sun; from your cloud bed arise;
Scatter the mist which lies in the valley
And makes every willow seem half its true size

Rip from the river the veils of morning
For ripples to glint where your early light falls,
And share with the flowers old meadows adorning
A tapestry varied as the dawn chorus calls

High Summer

In this the summer season of the sun
Fine days abolish any thought begun
To picture winter skeletons of trees
As other than faint lurking memories
Which dazzling hours obscure with the power
That from the demure bud will flaunt the flower.
Now in the fields the early corn displays
Its colour borrowed from these gilded days
And they rejoice together in the prime
Of wealth and beauty which is summertime,
But rung by rung death climbs the foxglove's stalk,
And poppy petals stain the garden walk
As if blood had been spilt there, and I find
Doom darkening the alley of the mind

La France

Mougins

To hosts in France with thanks for preservation in the land of my wife's dread

Once more my wife with greatest trepidation
Has let me journey to a foreign land
Where menace lurks, she says, at every station,
And bread is proffered with the unwashed hand;
Where men in fields give way to urination
On vegetables soon served by waiters bland;
Where women drench themselves and perspiration
With scent of cheap and nauseating brand;
Where milk in carts is drawn by dogs whose boredom
Will make them lift a leg against their wares;
Where certain bars hold out the lure of Sodom,
And many streets the brothel's busty snares.
How then do I survive this dreadful freedom
If not by my hosts' comprehensive cares?

Undressing On The Beach At Cannes

Where breasts and more are much exposed
I do not find it shocking
To show the world my veins are hosed
In one elastic stocking.

Letters To Mougins

In days too distant for me to redeem
I sent my letters to Alpes Maritimes,
And at those words my mind's eye saw sheep pass –
The wandering flock – through brown and ragged grass
Where tiny flowers made a Milky Way
And tinkling bell deceived the brazen day
With mimicry of cooling mountain stream.

Set high, like crags grown from the rock they own,
Old thick-walled villages of shuttered noon
Could hear the wandering bell and sighing pines
Beyond the terraced olives and the vines,
And smell sweet briar's scent and lavender's,
Which with the mistral's rage were visitors
To alleys secret from the searching sun.

Alas for memory! New villas flow
Across the land where olives used to grow;
Green lawns well watered in the summer's blaze
And golf course greens allow no flock to graze;
The bell is lost to air which car horns rend,
And no more to Alpes Maritimes I send
My letters, but to 06250.

Autumn, Alpes Maritimes

No longer fierce, an ageing sun
Is caged between back door and hedge,
Where plants in two small plots delay
Their final step at winter's edge –
Shall ripeness come before decay?

The peppers hang – misshapen moons –
Near yellowed leaves. Fig leaves are shed.
Tomatoes in their browning wrack
Deny the time, triumphant red,
Or greenly need the summer back.

The house cats find warm nooks at noon
Without a search. The old sun seeks
The daisies on the rain-fresh lawn,
But snow lies on the distant peaks
And evening cold stays after dawn.

November, Cote D'Azur

The emptiness of shuttered villas,
Their pale stained ochre walls
Unfired on dull days of November,
The yellowed leaf which falls,
Too tired for life, beside the pillars
Of padlocked gates – all these dismember
The summer empire of the sun,
And say that of my summers' number
One more is shuttered, padlocked, done.

Nice Under Rare Snow

Thick snow has overlaid the palms
Along the Promenade des Anglais
And smothered its constructed charms.
It is as if in bitter foray
Forgotten forces from the alps,
Untameable above the city,
Have served us notice that our scalps
Could still be taken without pity.

December 21st

The hilltop oak in late November,
Still flaunting all its russet leaf,
Seemed so to claim that autumn's ember
Would glow beyond belief,

And even into hard December
The creaking branches' clothes were there,
The brown leaves burnished into amber
In harsh bright winter air.

But glad eyes that had grown accustomed
To welcoming such bold display
Have opened to an oak uncostumed
On this the shortest day.

A Mystery of Nature

The mysteries of nature
Are still a vast domain
Where I shall never pasture
My slightly tutored brain.
Even in the countryside
Beneath a wing-crossed sky
I have not identified
Where dead birds' bones all lie.

Birds, Beasts & Insects

The 'Only Birds'

'Only a gull', the green-clad watcher sighed
And stepped back from her stand and telescope.
No triumph there, no prize identified,
But flown with distant gull the phantom hope.
Another 'only bird' – no albatross
From far patrol of seas which storms have stirred,
No snowy owl whose presence would be loss
To arctic shore. No; just an 'only bird'
Like 'only rooks', dark shapes on stubble wan,
Or 'only sparrows' bathing in warm dust,
Or 'only starlings' when sharp beaks rain down
To be the first to early morning crust.

The "Only Birds"

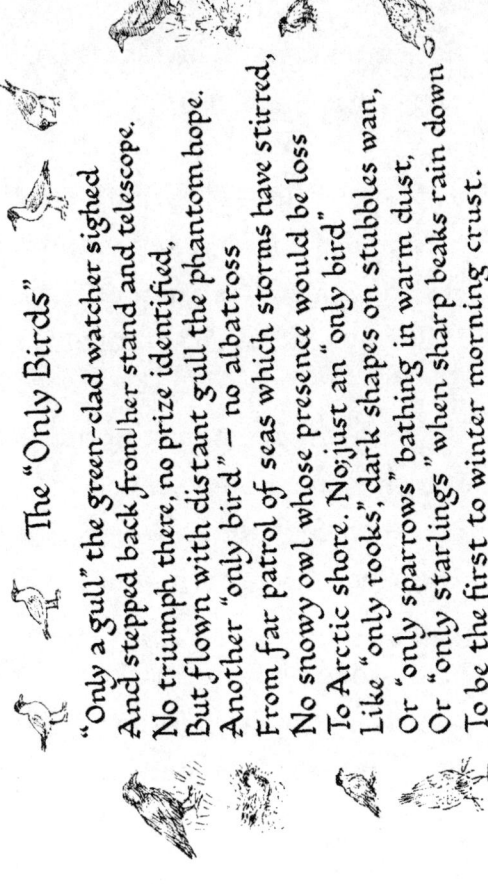

"Only a gull" the green-clad watcher sighed
And stepped back from her stand and telescope.
No triumph there, no prize identified,
But flown with distant gull the phantom hope.
Another "only bird" – no albatross
From far patrol of seas which storms have stirred,
No snowy owl whose presence would be loss
To Arctic shore. No; just an "only bird"
Like "only rooks", dark shapes on stubbles wan,
Or "only sparrows" bathing in warm dust,
Or "only starlings" when sharp beaks rain down
To be the first to winter morning crust.

Elegy For A Gannet

You beat the breast of Norfolk shore,
You cold grey sea of thudding wave,
But your lament will not restore
The broken gannet from its grave.

You mourn aloud in wind's attack,
Dark pines on sea-defying dune,
But this soiled feathered tideline wrack
Will never hear your keening tune.

No more the spearhead from the skies
Which pierced the sea in clean descent –
Like any stone the long beak lies.
The sand-clogged wings are random-bent.

No sodden feathers stir the air
Which sways the pines so noisily.
The eyes once keen in flight now stare
Unseeing at the blank North Sea.

The Nest Abandoned

Though trees were loath to come to bud
Till spring broke through an icy crust,
And though the towpath's rutted mud
Was stumble-hard, and summer dust
Undreamt, the swans began their nest –
A platform by the cold canal.
No more were they aloof: they hissed
At those who walked near their patrol.

In summer, when the waterway
Was rippled by the glinting wake
Of mallard's train, the swans' eggs lay
Unhatched, abandoned. One old drake
Lay sometimes by them but would keep
No vigil for the hopes of swans.
For him their nest meant rest and sleep
Which, with his food, were his concerns.

Farewell, Farewell

Your last call, cuckoo, - clear, clear sound
Across the wood and meadowland –
Has found me slow to understand
That in its first crisp note's rebound
This time the message was farewell.
I linger here to hear again
That double voice, but wait in vain
Among the fused small sounds which spell
A summer's quietness. Thrusting green
In spring once hid you, next the trees
Of darkened leaves. Now distant seas
Will be your mask, friend never seen.

Birds and Leaves

When gales toss birds about like leaves
Birds do not look like birds at all;
When leaves have long since had their fall
Their drab and sodden state deceives
The sight: one thinks of earth, not leaves.

When gales have gone the birds are seen
As birds again, and when the trees
Are dressed in stillness they will house
Behind their new leaves vivid screen
More birds to brave a winter's spleen

The Turning Earth

The moon which crossed my window said
Before the dawn that earth still turns,
But now that I am out of bed
My infant daylight sight discerns
No movement where the frost has spread
Grey sheets on autumn gold and browns.
The icy sun, its colour shed,
Freezes all the sky it burns
Until the starlings' rush for bread
Spins earth, and daily life returns.

Hard Winter

Cold, stiff, numb, almost skeletal,
The pigeon could not check its fall
From ice-caked branch to snow feet crunched.
At first it lay unmoving, hunched
And spent, then tried to flutter round
The tree. It could not leave the ground
And flopped again. The farmer's wife
Saw waif forlorn, not harvest thief.
She picked it up and stroked its head.
"The poor thing is so thin", she said.

When Martins Leave

Of birds which carved the summer air
Around our house in ebb and flow
Of sorties for their families' care
The martins are the last to go,
But start their long instinctive flight
While frost-free dahlias still glow
And dews make myriad points of light.
We wake one day to quiet and know
That from beneath abandoned eaves
Our tidy-mindedness will clear
The droppings which each family leaves.
The stubbles of East Anglia
Below the parting flight are turned,
And, rousing as the days draw in
And garden rubbish piles are burned,
The winter strokes a stubbled chin.

Snow In May

In meadows white the donkeys bray,
Surprised that there is snow today
So near the milder snows of May.

Their cries are echoed from the height
Of geese which pierce the early light
In sombre arrowhead of flight.

The arrows on the towpath show,
Imprinted backward in the snow,
Where hungry birds on searches go.

A Dog's Life

Of those dogs left to lie about
All day indoors or in a yard,
Or caged or kennelled on a hard
Dull concrete strip – left there without
Companionship of man or kind –
I wonder if their soul-filled eyes
Confound all efforts to disguise
A dreary lack of ways to find
The joys of sniffing nose-at-tail,
Or racing over grass leash-free,
Examining the scented tree
Or spurting signs along a trail.

Lioness

Morning Walks

On morning walks my eager bitch and I
Forsake the road and take the meadow path
Or follow the canal where upturned sky
Is patched with stretches of green weedy growth.
She celebrates her freedom from the lead
By hunting moles and sniffing long at grass
And running for the very joy of speed
While I look up to see the dark geese pass
In noisy skein, or note the change in trees
As seasons change, or watch the moorhen's walks
On water, or consider mysteries
Of journeys shown in snow by tiny marks.
My freedom is not from a leather lead
But from the subtle gadgetry of towns
Which poses as the essence of our need
And makes us into chattels which it owns.

Walks end. We find the waiting car and go
Back to the telly, fridge and radio.

To The Uttermost Forebear

Know this, old animal, now fossil bone
Embedded in a land you would find strange
If lost existence which was once your own
Were recreated by some magic change:
In our developed state you would not see
What science found beyond all memories' years –
Your groping, grunting, crude facsimile –
Though you are first in line of our forebears.

When first you walked upright then you began
The complicated progress which has led
To clever, fluent, gadget-master man,
But your old animal emotions bred
Through generations of our chemistry
Are now the substance of our poetry.

The Fox

Almost flamelike but revealed
In stillness where the blowsy wood
Spread autumn's embers by the field
The dog fox stood.

I, hidden where the bracken came
To field's edge, stood and watched him stay,
But soon he knew and like a flame
Flickered away.

Heat Wave

The dust spurts from the sparrows' bath,
The washing on the line hangs still,
Dust clouds engulf the combine's path
Cut through the barley on the hill
Beyond the paddock boundary.
By sieved sun flecked, the horses stay
In shade made by the widest tree,
And twitch and flick the flies away.
Blue distance quivers in heat's haze,
The cat sleeps long, the dog's tongue lolls,
Hot days succeed a month's hot days,
Leaves yellow early, no rain falls.

Cold Gold

Sky gold behind the skewbald trees
Whose green limbs white loads bear
Will not buy warmth for hands which freeze
In winter air.

The snow, though feather-soft to feel,
Is cruelly hard to those
Whose prints of pad and paw reveal
Where hunger goes.

The Ant And I

As I stand by the draining board
Above a darting ant I loom
And change from slave of greasy hoard
Of plates to god of ant, or doom.
Though tiny, it can sense or see
The menace of my thumb's descent.
The mystery which has made me
Has also made the minute ant.

Going and Coming

Wind tears the down from thistle heads,
Long yellow grasses bend,
The reeds writhe, raucous in their beds.
Is this the summer's end?
The godwits search the low-tide mud,
Back from their breeding site,
And soon a stirring in the blood
Will start the terns' long flight.
It will not now be long before
Geese cross a northern sea,
Land here, and in our minds restore
Migration's mystery

Flying Crooked

The butterfly, the cabbage- white,
(His honest idiocy of flight)
Will never now, it is too late,
Master the art of flying straight,
Yet has – who knows so well as I?
A just sense of how not to fly:
He lurches here and there by guess
And God and hope and hopelessness.
Even the aerobatic swift
Has not his flying-crooked gift.

Robert Graves

Requiem for a housefly

The fly is most companionable –
Now on my nose, now on my ear.
I brush it off but back it comes
Until I hit it on the table
Among the unswept breakfast crumbs,
And deep inside me shed a tear.

Not So Daft, Robert Graves

The cabbage white in flight behaves
Less foolishly than said by Graves,
For though it flutters here and there
With such inconsequential air
It uses all the airs that flow
To finish where it wants to go,
And from a course of dip and slant
Lands safely on its chosen plant.

Thoughts On Sundays

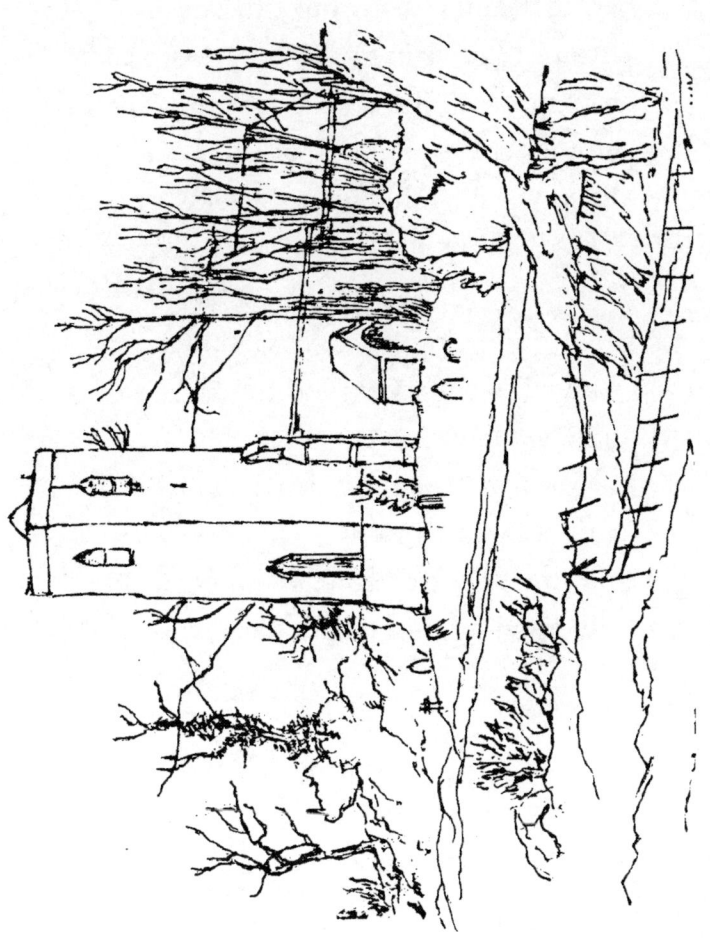

Chillesford Church

Sunday Service

Fresh flowers, this week in red and white, declare
The skill of Mrs. Smith. The two displays
Beside the altar draw our fitful gaze
Through chinks in fingers interlocked in prayer.
From brasses, tiles and speckless pews the care
Of other ladies shines to us who raise
Mixed voices thinly in our weekly praise
Of God and Sunday-best and well groomed hair.

How comforting it is, but, O, how far
From whiplash weals and from the thorn-
scratched brow,
The jeering crowd, the heat, the sweat, the jar
Of final steps on stony ways, the slow
And thirsty ebb of time, the opened skin
And crawling flies where nails were driven in!

Harvest Festival

When early hints of frost have gone
And young October days grow warm
The weekend motor mowers hum
A threnody from lawn to lawn
For greasy barbecues left cold
Through all the shorter days in sheds
Where cobwebs dim the light which spreads
On garden chairs and dust and mould.

But churches glow with fruit and flowers
While there the congregations sing
To praise the god of harvesting
For using those mysterious powers
Which fill the supermarket stores
With benefits of worldwide trade
When television screens parade
The fruits of drought and floods and wars.

Christmas Day

With little of the year to go
On weekdays at the kitchen sink
I saw beyond the garden fence
The hockey girls dash to and fro
With misty breath and faces pink
Till at the whistle's final blow
They trailed sticks to the lit school's glow
Across a darkening expanse.

Now at the sink on Christmas Day
I meet the unlit school's blank stare.
The meshes of the fence divide
A frosty playing field's display,
But gulls, not girls, are gathered there.
Not thought of much except today,
A girl long dead has halted play,
And hockey sticks are laid aside.

Progress

Before men first explored in outer space
Or bored beneath the once secretive sea,
When height and depth were each a mystery,
And of ourselves, confined by carapace
Of ignorance, we knew just mirrored face, not more -
Then love had not become biology,
And in our plunge towards our destiny
We did not dare to take the pilot's place.

Now love and hate, fear, destiny and hope
Are subjects of test tube and microscope.
The scope of science every year extends
Our own ability to shape our ends.
But God (if you be not the last illusion)
Preserve us from ourselves in that conclusion.

Great Gifts

The great gifts we were given were
Not gold and frankincense and myrrh
But questing mind and reasoning
And hands with skill for fashioning
The ideas of the questing mind
And so transforming humankind.

We saw mud dry, made pot and brick.
Stone, wood and bone gave us the trick
Of using tools. From things which roll
We took the idea of the wheel.
We tasted plants and found them good
And cultivated them for food.

In secrets of the air we found
New power, and deep in the ground,
And unconfined by bounds of birth
Have voyaged far beyond the earth.
We can amend genetic chains
And even manufacture brains.

And, almost masters of our fate
In concrete, steel and plastics state,
We use our skills to end disease
And spread disease in forest trees,

Our power to make the desert bloom
And make a desert of the blooms.

We aid the starving as we can
But can not stop man killing man;
We eat (with conscience ill at ease)
The victims of farm factories;
We advertise upon T.V.
The lures of greed and vanity.

A puzzle, this dichotomy.

Churchgoing

What superstitions have their thrones
Within these shaped and pitted stones
Beside which on each holy day
With others I have knelt to pray?

For centuries the tower bell
Called people here by whom the hell
Of priest and prayer book was more feared
Than lives of hardship which they shared.

Now I who come here cannot find
Belief in hell beyond the mind
And body. If that does not start
What value has its counterpart?

But here with my selective creed
I find, unhoping, peace I need,
Sing unconvinced of angel hosts
And kneel with my forefathers' ghosts.

Time

Is a river
Whose current, come from springs unknown,
Bears as driftwood
Our saplings to an unknown sea.

From Odiham Church walls

War

The Blitz

The light goes early; early frosts renew
On roof and grass their grey and glinting sheet.
In such chill seasons as the day withdrew
Fire-flickered windows signalled kitchen heat,
The singing kettle and the simmering stew;
The factory sirens called day's work complete
When, tugged on one by one, the gas lamps threw
Their soft-edged light into the dimming street.

The lamps are lit no more. The siren sings
A dirge in darkness to the windows void
In husks of homes. Death comes on bombers' wings,
And eyes turn upward from a street destroyed
To see, beyond the searchlights' probing bars,
The terrible remoteness of the stars.

1945

Lost men came into vision
When armistice made known
The secret darks of prison –
Came, grey skin over bone,
To find no more than shredding
Of flown but cherished years
While time prepared for shedding
Its opiates on tears.

Where Silence Tolls

Do not grieve only for this battle's dead.
Not even once will future's knife expose
Old agonies in them: the heart has fled;
The winter frost will find no waiting rose.
But in the fields where summer sweethearts tread
Their amber paths of happiness she goes
Alone and lonely from whom battle shed
In spring the summer which the lover knows.
In tidy rooms where silences will toll
The minute-weary passing of the year
She will engage herself in trivial toil,
Not hoping for a step upon the stair –
Till memory makes history of all
And time makes soft the hard sad lines of care.

After The Rhine

We drove away from battle's litter,
Leaving face and limb distorted;
Armour pitted, scorched and twisted;
Stiff-legged, swollen transport horses;
Guns mute; parachutes discarded,
Like flowers withered on a grave.

In pursuit we crossed a country
Into which slaves had been taken.
White sheets hung limply; furtive eyes
Peered out from homes of hidden fears;
But gaunt men frontiers from home
Wandered in confusing freedom
Like leaves loosed by a sudden gale.

Chances

War cannot without chancing choose
Which one to hit and which let live,
And so, in spite of martial plan,
The child unwarlike may still lose
More lifetime than the fighting man,
And pity slip through triumph's sieve.

Grief's Sullen Hammers

Grief's sullen hammers drive in many homes
The nails of bleakness through the future years.
No mortar bombs fall there on slit trench tombs,
And no mind trickles red its final fears,
But deeper than the thrust of bayonets
The bathroom's quietness wounds when morning comes,
And workers' steps which go past garden gates
Each night repeat the funeral beat of drums.

From Normandy

What soldiers' badges do we wear to war
Which differ from the scars of those whose wave
Was our farewell? Peace has no small enclave
For us to think of from a pitted shore.
Do risks we run outrun the risks they bore
Whom we have left? They were the hunted brave
Pursued by fire and falling architrave
In shells of towns.
Do we encounter more?
Not hunted but the hunters, we decide
To chase the quarry which may be our fate;
To take the next step where the mines are laid;
To dash across the enfiladed ride;
To search the cover where the Tigers wait
Or fingers clutch the desperate grenade.

Autumn Far From Balkan War

You weeping willow tree,
Your yellow tears now shedding,
Do not shed them for me.

The English autumn's splendour
Of red and gold array
Its riches must surrender
This damp and foggy day,
And in my mind engender
Faint tinges of dismay.

But could a summer taken
From one diminished store
Mean much to those lives stricken
In distant winter war,
Where home must be forsaken
And family known no more?

I do not have to scurry
At sirens' bleak alarms,
Go hungry, try to parry
The wielded rifle's harms.
I do not have to carry
A dead child in my arms.

The bright birch leaves make bedding
For mice. The carpetry
Of chestnut leaves is spreading.
You weeping willow tree,
Your yellow tears now shedding,
Do not shed them for me.

Time's Casualties

This morning martins flying swiftly south
Have passed above my roof. The swifts are gone,
And gone is every swallow; summer done;
The nest left empty in the eaves. Uncouth,
October's weather brings back home the truth
Of transience. The robin will be soon
The autumn friend once more to gardeners known.
The morning post has brought me news of death.

Old men have died whom I, at sixty-three,
Still see as young and brave in war, not old
And victims of an older enemy;
And I put on my winter vest (the cold,
You see) and play a record of the slow
Sad notes of Mozart's wind adagio.

The Last Despatch

Some lie in regimented grave,
Some left no more than just a name-
Fear- sharing soldiers who were brave –
While here I linger, stooping, lame
Not through the blows of battle's rage
But victim of undying foe:
Relentless, wrinkling, sapping age,
Which some I knew could never know.
Dialled numbers are not recognised;
I share a room with silent walls
And photographs by years disguised;
The postman hardly ever calls.

At The Time of Night Bombing of Cities

Let not cold images of carven stone
Be raised in memory of those who die
Like trampled flowers where the flesh and bone
Are shattered from their human symmetry.

As stone enduring is their troubled will.
From darkness screaming, bombs on homes descend,
And friends and family are lost, but still
These somehow face the threat of each day's end.

Who seeing heartless stone could also see
How hearts endured the long night's grim embrace?
A meet memorial for these would be
A humankind blessed with a kinder face.

Greenham Common Protesters

Encamped upon their muddy tract
At the missile base's border,
The Greenham ladies may distract
The police from keeping urban order,
And if engaging the police
Beyond their normal duty time
Do little for the cause of peace
And much more for the cause of crime.

Armistice Sunday

Rejoicing in the rare November sun,
Small children kick the tumbled leaves about,
And dash through them from tree to tree, and shout.
They do not know that webs of silence spun
By this bright day may seem to make it one
Just for the time when battle's ghosts come out
And in the ranks of memory's redoubt
Stand men who knew no children of their own.

No children's feet could be more profligate
With these dead leaves than humankind with lives.
What can we do but try to reinstate
In this last refuge which our thought contrives
The hopes of those who were so young when killed,
So early dammed, and ever unfulfilled?

Brief Reunion

We take them out and make them shine –
Our medals and our memories –
Just once each year, and you in line
March out from long closed histories
Who were unlucky or just brave.
You dug latrines, you cleaned the Bren,
Patrolled, were mortared, found your grave.
Now we patrol with you again
But draw back from a distant war
And shut the turret top once more.

Veterans' Reunion

They come to London once each year –
These men with grey and thinning hair,
Long pants to keep out autumn cold,
And cheap rail tickets for the old.

They meet. They shake arthritic hands,
And wince. They tell of prostate glands,
But to each other make quite clear
That looks have fooled another year.

In conversation when they dine
They mention battles near the Rhine,
But in this talk interpolate
New details of their families' state.

Grandchildren's welfare means much more
Than fading memories of war
To these whose fellowship began
In hiding fear and fighting man.

Thus men who dashed from Orne to Seine
Past reddened hulks and bloated slain,
And watched the shadows' menace pass
From bitter nights beside the Maas

Leave early for the homeward train.

DUNKIRK VETERANS

With a Dunkirk rescue boat behind them, on Loch Lomond, two Dunkirk veterans, Ken Jenkins and Bryan White, at a reunion of the 15th Scottish Reconnaissance Regiment, with which they had returned to fight again in France

Suffolk

King's Farm, Westleton

Suffolk

From Suffolk mariners can sail
To all the seven seas,
And boats tossed by the Arctic gale
Know calm beside our quays,
And there are men who cannot rest
While there is still a store
Of new experience to test
Far from the Sandlings' shore.

But those who chose adventure's cloak
Have left no wardrobe bare,
For Suffolk pine and crooked oak
Are homespun clothes to wear
With barley and the muddy beet,
Marsh, heath and shingle strand –
Experience enough to suit
Those folded by this land.

Who walks in Melton's winter wood
Can treasure silver bars
Where trunks divide the Deben's flood.
In summertime he hears
No tune more soothing than the tide
Whose blue inflow expands
Alde's narrow channel from Snape's side
To Iken's secret sands.

When autumn brings its fiery change,
Though dark aisles stay aloof,
Old trees in orange glow outrange
The pantiled farmhouse roof,
And when the green flames leap in spring,
Or fields are starred in flower,
What better place for wandering
Than meadows by the Stour?

Our East Coast estuaries' mud
Spreads wide a satin sheen
Which waders print in search of food,
And leave for tides to clean
Whose waves on rough days try to rear
To low banks' cloudy crowns
And calmer reaches through the year
Are elegant with swans.

Behind those banks reedbeds reply,
Low-voiced, to North Sea's call
Beneath the same unhindered sky
Much loved by Constable
Which dapples marsh where cattle graze
In distances remote
By dykes in which the ends of days
Find early moons afloat.
Go west to clay and barley song,

Where men wove Kersey's name
And built great towers which belong
To God but still proclaim
The wealth of wool, and Bury's stones,
Like mounds and children's hair,
Are mute reminders that our bones
Are Dane's and Saxon's heir.

Go north to crumbling cliffs which fail
To halt the hard sea's course,
And dawn wakes to a fairy tale
Of gossamer on gorse,
And stand and watch the rabbits run,
The far treed miles unfold,
High on the heath at Westleton,
And shake the hand of God.

East Suffolk

The tall and dark pine forests guard
The crossbills' haunts with ramrod trees,
And old, arthritic woods discard
Their leaves on leaves of centuries.
Low sandy cliffs and shingle shore
Fight age-old battles with the sea,
Advancing here, here yielding more
Where boats sail over history.
On heaths the early sun will find,
When sea mists go, the yellow blaze
Of gorse, and where broad rivers wind
Through marshes dots of cattle graze,
So small beneath vast skies. They share
Their long and low and lonely land
With seabird, peewit, lark and hare.
On river heights the mounds still stand
Where Saxons had their burials
But left their blood to flow in veins
Of pretty, soft-tongued Suffolk girls,
And in the barley-bordered lanes –
Once paths their Saxon forebears trod –
Old men of country dignity,
Perched high on bicycles as old,
Ride slowly to eternity.

May Morning, Westleton Heath

The mist came cold in from the sea;
Quite still, the heath in silence lay
But for the nightingale's decree,
Throbbed out, that this was May.

The sun, like one late out of bed,
Peered through the muslin of the mist,
And morning's reticence was shed
And hidden life released.

The bee flies on its zig-zag course
Where heather spreads, the butterfly
Jinks brightly where the yellow gorse
Grows brighter with the sky.

The sunshine fires the linnet's breast,
The blackbird sings and insects hum
On unseen ways, and all attest
That May indeed has come.

Adlestrop *But not of Suffolk!*

Yes. I remember Adlestrop –
The name, because one afternoon
Of heat the express train drew up there
Unwontedly. It was late June.

The steam hissed. Someone cleared his throat.
No one left and no one came
On the bare platform. What I saw
Was Adlestrop – only the name

And willows, willow- herb, and grass,
And meadowsweet, and haycocks dry,
No whit less still and lonely fair
Than the high cloudlets in the sky.

And for that minute a blackbird sang
Close by, and round him, mistier,
Farther and farther, all the birds
Of Oxfordshire and Gloucestershire.

Edward Thomas

I Remember Adlestrop

One man, a stranger there and long since dead,
His lines on one June day, one train's brief stop,
Had set eternal summer in my head,
But they were all I knew of Adlestrop
Until by chance at Evenlode I read
The name upon a signpost, and was drawn
To homes the tint of lightly crusted bread,
Where few birds thrilled the heart of August's noon.

The station board, become the village sign,
Announced its houses, tended, spruce, discreet;
A man was polishing a smart car's shine
In tidy street. Somehow it seemed more meet
To memory that one old cyclist rode
Back, scarecrow-like, to unsung Evenlode.

From Clamour to Curlew Call

When buffeted in busy streets
And surfeited and dulled by all
The noisy bustle which defeats
The senses, so that tops of tall
Unfriendly buildings crumble clouds
Unseen, and no one step is heard
Among the steps of hurried crowds.
And mouths are dumb, and faces blurred,
And nostrils fail to analyse
The mixture of the city's fumes –
Then I recall wide Suffolk skies,
The rustle of the reedbeds' plumes,
The waddling shelducks' sharp design –
White, black and brown -, their printed trails
Where tides have left Alde's mud to shine
And curlews make their haunting calls.

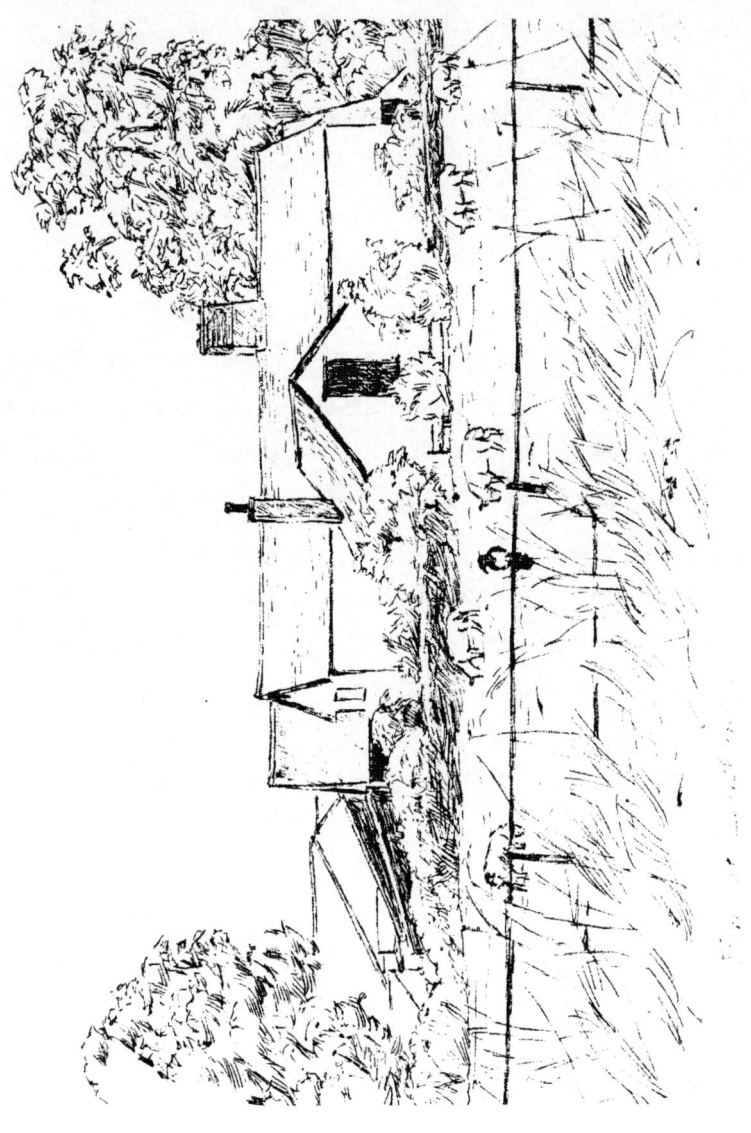

Farm at Darsham

Abbey Ruins At Minsmere

These lonely ruins are not really sad,
Though set as if to stage a tragedy:
By wide marsh girdled and dim evening clad
Between the west's red fringed and darkened wood
And slow pulse of the mournful-sounding sea.

Their flint walls do not feel the brambles' claws
Where brambles pierce the shadows of their mound,
Nor do they heed the breaker's thump and pause,
Or in the quietness when the wave withdraws
Detect the restless reed bed's softer sound.

They do not brood on ages of decline;
No hope of theirs was dashed with fallen stone;
Flaws cause them no regret; they see no sign
Of ravages to come; they do not pine
For times long past. Their sadness is my own.

By Dunwich Shore

A high steep bank of shingle hides
The marsh from unrelenting tides;
The piled-up pebbles, brown and grey,
Appear to keep the seas at bay,
And strangers may not know that these
Are hungry and devouring seas.
Beneath them lies a crumbled town;
This mottled marsh itself may drown.

The peewits here, alarmed, protest
In circles when I near their nest;
The hare, alert before I pass,
Is soon a trail of waving grass;
The skylark runs before my feet –
None knows of time's remoter threat,
And in my thoughts alone reeds brood
In dark expectancy of flood.

But though it is my mind which braves
The future I can not be more
Than one small pebble in the waves
Which strike and shift the rampart shore.

Thames Barge   *Sailing to Ipswich*

Her sails of tan taut in a westerly breeze,
She hurried along on the outflowing tide
Which raced to the welcome of wind-whitened seas
Where Thames, Swale and Medway make one their last stride.

She came from the pool and its crowded display
Of barge, lighter, derrick, mast, funnel and shroud.
She went a red smear in remote skyline grey
Where look-outs see little but dull scudding cloud,

The sea, and the seagull in purposeful flight,
The coast long and low, and a tramp dipping by
With blown trail of smoke as she crosses the sight –
From sky come to water, from sea gone to sky.

The Fens in Winter

The drained fens plead a winter poverty
And hide dark riches from the filtered light
In flatness stretching to obscurity.
Few trees obstruct the wind, each in its height
A peak of loneliness on shrinking earth.
Remains of crops and new crops' first faint signs
Make patterned rectangles of death and birth
Which distance narrows until each resigns
Its blurred identity. No hedges stand
To shelter birds, and every brimming drain
In menace draws a long, straight livid band
Across the sunken patchwork of the sunken plain.

Spring Ploughing

The late snowflakes which feathered
Stack, silo, clamp and barn
Have lain, grown grey and gone,
And snowdrops have delivered
White hints of spring. Gulls now,
From sea's rough wakes untethered,
Are wakes behind the plough.

Marshes

Each marsh that I have known displays
The looks of others. Each recedes
On levels crossed by waterways
Whose whispering wind-ruffled reeds
Accompany the skylark's song
And curlew's intermittent call
Which makes space sad. Perhaps along
Some inland edge daylight's last fall
Is snared by woods already dark
Before night steals the background hills
And, nearer, casts its masking cloak
On sheep and settled geese, and fills
The creeks where tidal waters creep.
Yet in my thoughts no rays of dawn
Caress the reed or stir the sheep
Except hard by where I was born
And where I first breathed salt marsh air
When as a child I went to play
By ragged ewes and peewits there-
In years and miles now far away.

Odds & Ends

Weather Forecasts

Weather charts on television
Shape the day with trim precision;
The forecaster's account is
Of physical geography.
But now October's charted gales
Leap living from the west to me.
They hurl great waves at Cornish walls
And wrestle, howling, every tree
Across eight southern counties
And cry again lost ancient calls
Round Dorset's rampart mystery.

The Lights Of May

The daisies welcome cow parsley,
Cow parsley winks at may,
The candles of the chestnut tree
Add light to sunny day,
And I who heavy-heartedly
Sought years long gone astray
Now in May's mild snow mimicry
Go lighter on my way.

So Idly Drifts the Severed Leaf

So idly drifts the severed leaf
Across a sky of unconcern
In grey December that belief
Can hardly hold that its return
From tree to earth is purpose-bent,
But, rotted on the woodland floor,
It will provide the nourishment
On which new eager life will draw.

As we draw nearer to our pyre
By twists and turns decreed by fate
And not the path of our desire
What purpose can the world relate,
Uncaring, to our wandering?
Will scattered ash – or word or deed
Before that final scattering –
Invigorate some future seed?

Out On My Walk

Out on my walk one blessed day
The scales built up by many years
Of life's compelling feats and fears
From my dulled eyes were stripped away,
And grass no longer was just grass
But tiny beads on slender tethers,
Green whiskers, spearheads, sheaths and feathers
That sway whenever breezes pass –
The long lost friends of childhood's eye.
Then scent gave back the random rose
And opened ears heard winds disclose
The inmost secrets of the tree.

Knotty Problem

In childhood, with worlds to explore
Within me and without,
To tie shoe laces was a chore
Quite hard to carry out.
With life become a well worn track
And little left unknown
That childhood problem has come back
To fingers clumsy grown

Night

Night is not only darkness which enfolds
Familiar beds more closely than the womb,
And from eyes dulled by coming sleep withholds
The friendliness of shapes which make up home.
Night is not only city centre's glares
Or light which leaps from pubs when drinkers go,
Or muggers waiting on the unlit stairs
Of tower blocks to strike a furtive blow.

Outside the curtains and the light bulb's bounds
A small bird shifts beside the frosted thorn,
And double in the distant darkness sounds
The vixen's cry, and forest fears are born,
And where we left the litter of our spoors
Night's darkened seas scrub clean our sullied shores.

Abandoned Line

A little train would leave its lingering trail
Where rosy oasts exhaled the dried hops' scent.
Its white smoke echoed each white steepling cowl
And made its distant journey evident
As silver shows the progress of a snail
On mossed brick paths, but now the smoke is spent:
No halt abandons sleep at whistled hail,
No hissing wait disturbs a quiet content.

The train now crosses only memory's weald
In sunshine which the dusk alone revokes.
From dawn mist there tall elms, unblighted, rise,
Astir with rooks, and in the noon's bright field
Red cattle bunch beneath wide spreading oaks,
And horses nod away the clustered flies.

Season Signals

Six leaves - three orange and three red
Warm colours against smudgy clouds,
Hang limp as signs that days ahead
Will wrap us in cold winter shrouds
To have, when north and east winds stir
Bare trees by times austere design,
The company of sombre fir
Unchanged, and still the dark-clad pine

Shopping In December

I carried shopping slowly home
Along with sixty-seven years,
And at each step grew more aware
That things which, picked from shelves, seem light
Together seem too much to bear.

Potatoes, carrots, liquid foam
For washing-up, tinned soups and pears,
Bread, marmalade and rich fruit cake,
Eggs, margarine – when they unite
Then shoulders sag and fingers ache.

December's wind hurt like a comb
In tangled hair, my eyes grew tears
And droplets gathered at my nose,
But as I passed a garden's plight
I saw one pink and perfect rose.

Costly Goal

If you are panting up the slope
Which leads from childhood's leisured plain,
Your eyes fixed firmly on the top,
Your hope that there you will attain
The plateau of a magic land,
Just pause sometimes before the crest
Is reached and see what is at hand,
For at the summit you may find
That some of life that is the best
Was in the slope you left behind

Bottled Plums

How prudent is the mind which can foresee
In velvet hours of late summer glory
The bone-bare time when summer's wealth shall be
Remembered as a half forgotten story!

Tonight I breathe the orchard's winey scent
And gaze in idleness at glowing stars
While others' hands in laboured hours are spent
That bottled plums may gleam within their jars.

Arts Council Grants

On those high planes of culture
Which governments support
The intellectual vulture
Lands often with the thought
That pickings from that carcass
Are far short of enough,
Which really should concern us
For we provide the stuff.

It may be deemed a measure
In which good sense is scant
To subsidise the pleasure
To do just what they want
Of men of arts whose vision
May not improve the mind
And never can provision
The bellies of mankind.

People

Martin Weston Eve

Daughters And Mothers

A celebrated woman writes
Of famous mother that her nights,
No matter when or even where,
Were times for washing underwear,
So, women, if you scale a peak,
Write novels or high office seek
And wish to be remembered so
Take care that when and where you go
You always at the end of days
Wash smalls safe from small daughter's gaze.

Message To My Daughters

My daughters, I explored this continent
To which you voyage from the harbour womb.
Where you make landfall you will see the frame
Of my abandoned caravel; the hint
Of far-off camp fires on the land wind's scent
Will draw you inland. How can I assume
The role of marker-guide that you find home
With ease on trails of my experiment?

But no, I cannot, for the deserts shift,
The jungles spread and rivers alter course.
You will not see the cairn which I have left
To mark the pass. Your triumph and your loss
Must come to you through your discovery
And you, alone, cross your last boundary.

Stars in the Hedge

Pity the child who never knows
That stars come down to earth
And shine here as the pale hedge rose
To celebrate June's birth

A Mother's Memory

The doctor said my child should not remain
Inside me longer for its sake and mine.
Indeed, for both our sakes out it must come
Some weeks before it should desert the womb.
So it was done, with no caesarean used –
They were rare then – but painfully induced.
A boy, weak, tiny. I could not but think
Of monkeys. Was that wrong? He could not drink
His milk from me: cleft palate and hare lip
Made that too hard. We had no modern drip
To strengthen him. We struggled with pipette
And kept him going for four months, and yet
That could not be enough. All my others,
They grew up fine – sisters, yes, and brothers.

Grey, widowed, stout, already short of breath,
And she herself not many years from death,
She spoke quite calmly, with a hint of old,
Now softened, sadness in the story told.

Values

Not now to know great cities of the world,
The farthest island or the frozen peak,
Or hold the world's attention when you speak
And claim a little place in history
Or headline banner by the mind soon furled –
Is this a humdrum destiny to rue
In terraced homes beside gasometers
Where neighbours known by name share growing old,
Or in the long suburban avenue
Where almond trees are spring's interpreters,
Or seeing every day the wind-whipped tree
Set high above the valley's sheltered waters,
Or hearing on the worn and scrubbed threshold
Familiar steps of growing sons and daughters.

Beauty Borrowed

The swan engraved on summer water
Seems still as swans of porcelain,
But drift unheeded sets it later
Against a new reflected green.

The bee upon the thistle's purple
Seems settled to the casual eye
But even then its wings uncouple
A perfect jewelled harmony.

Your curving cheek, your brow unforrowed –
O! cherish them while hours chime.
On such smooth beauty, briefly borrowed,
Descends the graving tool of time.

Young And Old

An autumn poster on the barn
Proclaims a newly calven cow,
And that is all; the rest has gone,
Torn off by some north-easter's blow.

But spring has come to winter's bones,
And on a nearby garden wall
A child explores the pitted stones
In sunshine, with no haste at all.

A lifetime waits for her to grow.
An old man, leaning on his stick,
Inspects the earth; he wants to sow
The crop which he may never pick.

Ancestors

Men who sweated lives away in sawpits
And added aches to years,
Men whose lungs the dust destroyed in coalpits,
Brave men who took their fears
With sail and oar to fish in wayward seas,
The men who trod the clay
To plough between their headland boundaries
Day after numbing day,
Their wives made old when young by children bred
Too often and by cares
And need for miracles with meagre bread –
Such were our ancestors.
As children some picked stones much more than flowers,
And some old fading lives
Were slowly dragged through aimless workhouse hours,
Men separate from wives.

Waiting To See The Doctor

Dull-eyed, secretive, coughing, drawn,
We stare at homes in Country Life
Which are too grand for us to own,
But think about the length of life.
We study other people's shoes.
We wonder if another's face
Will yield to furtive search the clues
To what has brought her to this place.
A wife and husband, close, confide
Their low-toned trivialities
Of daily things which do not hide
Their unexpressed anxieties.
Young children chatter without fear
Across the doctor's waiting room;
Their voices through the tension rear
Like cockerels' calls on days of gloom.

Looking At A Stately Home

We stand before the house and supplement
Our first impressions with what Pevsner says:
Late Georgian, eight bays, a pediment,
Pilasters, portico and terraces.
But dry facts listed and a bland façade
Reveal no secrets of the building's life,
No homely hopefulness, no feelings hard,
No tenderness, no stress of family strife.
We cannot hear the child's first thrilling cry
Or see the old hand feebly stroke the sheet
As breathing weakens and last hours slip by.
No bricks can make us sense the moment sweet
When hearts and minds and blood would all unite
In sudden chord of harmony. Who knows
The romance of the vanished summer night
When nostrils were beguiled by scent of rose,
Or who worked long among the kitchen smells –
The greens, the grease, the appetising airs –,
Whose bare chapped hands picked up the frosty pails,
Whose ageing feet grew tired on dark back stairs?

Bays, pilasters and pediment,
Date, terraces and sometimes towers –
In guide books thus the sediment
Of dreams and hopes and long sobbed hours.

Dogdays

Along brick canyons cats absorb
Unblinkered sun on burning sills.
The wireless sets and flies disturb
Hot silence round the kitchen smells.
The old, old men sit statue-still
But stir to spit. Dogs move with shade.
Young children fret, and women fill
Their years too soon and fade.

The Fireside Men

The morning shadows on the road
Were frostless hints that now were gone
Grey days when draughts pierced homes like spears
And sleet in its relentless code
Tapped out again unpleasant truth,
And fireside men looked back on years
That faded into far-off youth
And thought of things they had not done.

Now sunlit silences explode
With cockerels' cries, the slanting grass
Is light beneath the lark's high song,
And now the old men's steps are slowed
Not by their weakness but desire
To stay where memories belong,
And faint within their hearts a fire
Denies that all of youth must pass.

In Bond Street

Though more than youth has gone,
She stands and stares
At underwear with artfulness displayed
To conjure visions of young limbs arrayed
In clinging silk, and breasts whose shape declares
Sweet curves of youth through lacy brassières.
All artifice can do has been her aid –
Dyes, lotions, massaging – yet here, dismayed,
She lingers, mocked by these expensive wares.

Go, woman, go! Let time's calligraphy
Describe you now. Search out the decent black
Of peasant widows, and with dignity
Accept grey hairs. But this resolve you lack,
For growing old has as its hardest part
That flesh will wither round the youthful heart.

At Victoria Station

Why do you cry beside the platform gate?
You do not seem to say a sad goodbye
Unless it be to youth belatedly,
Tall woman, middle-aged, in jeans too neat.
Your costumed woman friend, disconsolate
But disconcerted, stands by silently,
And fitful dabbings at your tearful eye
Alone your miseries communicate.

Trains come and go. The jerky pigeon strides
In crumb search round your feet, all unaware
Of your distress. No traveller provides
The crumbs to comfort you, for who can care
About your fate as swift commuting tides
Swirl round your lonely island of despair?

Darts Match

No heroes now, no rogues, no types of men,
But flesh forgotten and unheeded heart,
Mind lost to thought, and eye that will not part
From one round board so brightly lit, but then
An arm will move, a hand release the dart
And free in each his character again.

Commuters' Homeward Train

We travel breast to back and thigh to thigh,
Confined by speed and circumstance, become
Close pressed as rugby forwards in a scrum,
But never intimate. The searching eye
Can find no eye's companionship; the cry
Unuttered beats against the shuttered room
Of mind and heart. We are apart and dumb
While lighted homes, unreticent, flash by.

Because our night train's passing is for them
So much part of their lives they do not veil
Their nakedness by any stratagem.
Each lighted window tells its dumb-show tale
In swift vignette and into night is gone
While we rush onward, crowded, masked, alone.

Man And Crow

The man who walked before me to his train
Was dark against the freshly fallen snow –
Dark shoes turned outward and dark coat, dark hat,
Dark briefcase which the City's needs explain;
Yes, dark and jerky as a walking crow.
No natural grace moved in his overcoat.

Unlike the crow, he never can disdain
Earth's ties without the help of some machine,
And soar away from awkwardness at whim;
But his snug house keeps out the snow and rain,
Has plumbing and the television screen.
No gibbet, poison, shotgun bother him.

If You Go Back

If you go back to any well loved place
Long in the gallery of pictured past
You see the lines engraved upon the face
Remembered smooth, and hear the voice which cast
Its treble confidence on morning's reach
Grown strident with the tones disguising doubt
Or falter huskily at night's approach.
Where you will knock the householder is out.

You will not meet your youth in men grown grey
Or women now the grandmothers' of girls,
And all your talk will be of yesterday.
The hand which stiffly by the bank uncurls
Will find in waters once of richer yield
No mirrored silver for the empty field.

A Golden Day

Gold- turning reeds wave feathered heads
And dance above their dancing twins
While, in their shelter, water threads
Its way between soft-singing beds
To where the marshland edge begins.

In breeze so clean, in light so clear,
Though time has loosened summer's hold
It brings to us these moments dear
When silver birches, neighbour- near,
Toss to the reeds their glints of gold.

Sunbathers In May

The trees have set their fullest sail,
And summer's seas come flooding in.
Cow parsley is the verge's surf,
And daisies in the park's warm turf
Are glints of waves around the pale
Sprawled islands of the winter skin.

On Tankerton Sea Front

Now talking of bottoms of backs,
While some may be suited by slacks
It is a gross error, I think,
To clad thus two big wobbles in pink.

Country And Town

The person in the village street
May well be one whom you will greet
And see entire and understand –
A fellow creature of your land.

The passers-by in city streets
May well be fragments no one greets –
The friendly eye has gone astray;
There is no time for time of day.

Looks and Feeling

I see old men about the street
Bent, grey, lined, hesitant of feet,
And seldom does it seem to me
That I have lived more years than they,
Though every morning now I shave
A mirrored face I did not have,
And if I brave the Underground
Young women lately I have found
Not linking me with youth's heartbeat,
Stand up and offer me their seat.

Time's Legacy

Time has seen the Romans
Wade onto Sussex shore,
And the English bowmen's
Shafts rain at Agincourt
And Time with its unfaltering tread
Abandoned them, the unknown dead.

Time watched empires fatten
And next their powers wane -
The trading posts of Britain,
The treasure chests of Spain.
Time saw their fortune's downward turn
And went away without concern

Time's disguise for childhood
Seems to extend its hours
So that each young gaze could
Find wonder in small flowers,
But children's hustled future lies
Beyond the bounds of Time's disguise.

Time passes those who find
Their adult lives too full
To be, when needed, kind
And always honourable,
And while the world their acts forgets
Old men live last with their regrets.

Frank Woolley, cricketer

died October 1978

Though I regard your passing with regret,
It is part selfish, for your death must cull
That boyhood part of me whose eyes were met
On Kentish grounds by strokes so masterful
From graceful bat that no field could be set
To make a hazard for the speeding ball.
A county's summer pride – few will forget
The jewelled deeds of which your days were full.

Mean caution scorned, your shots were never made
For averages. The glory of your powers
Was all your team's. With modesty you played,
And in the story of the games two layers,
When one was amateur, the other paid,
You are the very gentleman of players.

September

The fields of summer, harvested and bare,
Stretch palely to low hedge and lofty tree
Which move but little in the languid air
And in their dark green uniformity
Wait like full-bosomed matrons, queuing there,
Not for May's tender varied finery
But one last fling of henna for the hair
Before the months of stark anatomy.

We wait for pensions in post office queues
At our own summer's end, some short, some tall,
But much alike in sober clothes we choose
And hair grown grey, and sometimes we recall
The quivering thrill of our now distant May
When steps were light, hair gleamed and clothes were gay.

The Divide

It was the hand which made me stare,
A hand at such an awkward angle
That one might think a puppeteer
Had left it so with strings a tangle.

But it was not the hand alone
Which human symmetry disclaimed
But shoulder of lopsided bone
And leg that was for ever lamed.

Of what peninsular of pain
Was that bent hand the farthest cape?
What tempests of despair had brain
Endured in that warped body's shape?

The answers I can only guess,
For he, a stranger, stranger stayed.
I who could cross a mountain pass
Could not cross over that divide.

What's To Come?

Where lamplight wavers
Against the skulking shadow of the wall
Stand clutched the lovers.
What whispers fall
From lips which scarcely move
Except to seal their love?
Perhaps he breathes of Helen or compares
Her beauty to a summer's day;
Perhaps some old sad song she airs –
Take, O! take, those lips away.

They do not think of mornings
When ashes are cold in the grate,
And rain lashes
The hand that feels for the milk bottle,
The baby is sick,
The rent a month late,
And passion grown cold as the ashes.

Edwin (Ted) Bell (1921-1992)
Cathedral chorister, Kings Scholar, Victor Ludorum,
wartime soldier, journalist, author, sports editor,
deputy editor of Eastern Daily Press

In Memoriam, E.B.

An autumn comes which tells a different tale:
No more the future seed and harvest seem
The whispered secret in the shouting gale;
No gold unspent is in the wrenched leaf's gleam.
The worn joints creak which raucous winds abuse;
The red blackberry withers by the thorn
Like hope which never ripens, and the dews
Are moist as tears upon the ragged lawn.

So many autumns in their richness wear
The proof and promise of renewing spring,
But one arrives and other facts lays bare:
First details of a final reckoning.
The new young frost foretells the old life's end,
And rough winds blow away a lifetime friend.

In Memoriam, M. W. E.

It was the time of the carting of the beet.
The gale was strong from the south-west,
And breakers reared against The Sandlings' shore.
Leaves chased the fleeing clouds.
The reeds writhed in their beds,
And in the boatyards
Rigging sang the song you knew so well.
And you had sailed safely to your haven.

In time and place this was appropriate
Because you had returned before too late
Into the countryside whose stamp you bore;
Whose many waters you had sailed before
You braved in youth the savage seas of war;
The land whose natural music was your own consort
While, playing old church organs, yours matured;
And where, undaunted by disease, you sought
Mankind's salvation by the published word.

Martin Weston Eve (1924-1998): cathedral chorister, pianist, wartime seaman and naval officer, founder of Merlin Press and Seafarer Books.

Thoughts In A Bath (or not T. S. Eliot)

Snug in his nook, Great-Uncle Herbert
Was sucking from a bag of sherbert
Through its short black liquorice tube.
"My boy, this beats a sugar cube,"
He said, "you'll find it tastes as fine
At ninety as it did at nine.
Now when I was a boy at school
A penny sherbet was the rule,
And for our penny we could choose
The tube or toffee dab to use
For taking it. At last I find
Another bag. O! Life is kind."
Mum, patient, gazed up at the ceiling,
Then "Men!" she sighed with such deep feeling.

> Trying in my bath to remember more of that verse by A. P. Herbert, somehow my thought wandered to "The Waste Land", and somehow this doggerel was the incongruous result!

Putting On Socks

In days when I scampered through spring's meadow plants,
Feet then even of sandals free,
Bunions were hallmarks of elderly aunts.
Now corns are the hallmarks on me.

The Octagenarian

The troubles that descend on men
Have come to me more now than then.
What once seemed heartache's misery
Proved merely passing fantasy,
But now new weaknesses increase
As time trots on to my decease,
And I encounter every day
More evidence of mind's decay.
Sometimes on entering a room
I cannot think why I have come
And to discover why must trace
My steps right to their starting place;
Familiar names escape my tongue;
Keys hide from where they should belong;
And I must go back more and more
To make sure I have locked a door.
From company I may depart
Too late to cloak the urgent fart;
I ache when I get out of bed;
I walk down slopes with timid tread;
But amid the twinges felt,
Names forgotten, words mis-spelt
Old blemishes I would forget
Are vivid and steadfastly set.

01.01.2001

Though long dead voices are not heard,
Mind speaks to mind through printed word;
The brush strokes made in former days
Disclose to us the artist's ways;
And notes of a familiar strain
Bring thought back from a vanished brain.
In concerts, books and galleries
We leap across the centuries.
And now what? In the years to come
Will someone press with casual thumb
A button, and see us revealed
With all time's layers from us peeled,
And find out that in spite of change
Some thoughts and feelings are not strange